UNDERSTANDING DISEASE
AND WELLNESS
Kids' Guides to Why People Get
Sick and How They Can Stay Well

A KID'S GUIDE TO DRUGS & ALCOHOL

VILLAGE EARTH PRESS

Series List

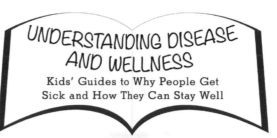

UNDERSTANDING DISEASE
AND WELLNESS
Kids' Guides to Why People Get
Sick and How They Can Stay Well

A KID'S GUIDE TO DRUGS & ALCOHOL

Chance Parker

Understanding Disease & Wellness:
Kids' Guides to Why People Get Sick and How They Can Stay Well
A KID'S GUIDE TO DRUGS & ALCOHOL

Village Earth Press
Vestal, NY 13850
www.villageearthpress.com

First Printing
9 8 7 6 5 4 3 2 1

Series ISBN (paperback): 978-1-62524-445-1
ISBN (paperback): 978-1-62524-412-3
ebook ISBN: 978-1-62524-047-7
    Library of Congress Control Number: 2013911240

Author: Parker, Chance.

Introduction

According to a recent study reported in the Virginia Henderson International Nursing Library, kids worry about getting sick. They worry about AIDS and cancer, about allergies and the "super-germs" that resist medication. They know about these ills—but they don't always understand what causes them or how they can be prevented.

Unfortunately, most 9- to 11-year-olds, the study found, get their information about diseases like AIDS from friends and television; only 20 percent of the children interviewed based their understanding of illness on facts they had learned at school. Too often, kids believe urban legends, schoolyard folktales, and exaggerated movie plots. Oftentimes, misinformation like this only makes their worries worse. The January 2008 *Child Health News* reported that 55 percent of all children between 9 and 13 "worry almost all the time" about illness.

This series, **Understanding Disease and Wellness**, offers readers clear information on various illnesses and conditions, as well as the immunizations that can prevent many diseases. The books dispel the myths with clearly presented facts and colorful, accurate illustrations. Better yet, these books will help kids understand not only illness—but also what they can do to stay as healthy as possible.

—*Dr. Elise Berlan*

Just the Facts

- People use drugs and alcohol for many different reasons. They may use drugs or alcohol to get away from their problems, to fit in with people who drink or use drugs, or because they want to feel differently than they normally do. There is no one reason that people use drugs, but there are many reasons not to.

- Using drugs or drinking alcohol can hurt your body and keep you from doing the things that you love to do. Drugs and alcohol can damage young people's health and change their lives in many negative ways.

- There are drugs that are against the law to use and drugs that are helpful to people all over the world. The medicines you take when you are sick are kinds of drugs that are legal and helpful. Drugs like cocaine, heroin, and others are against the law and don't have any helpful effects.

- Abusing drugs and alcohol can lead to addiction. Addiction is what happens when the body starts to need drugs or alcohol, making a person who is addicted feel like they have to drink more or take more of the drug they are addicted to.

- If you or someone you know has a problem with drugs or alcohol, there are many ways to stop using and get help. There are many kinds of treatments for people who have problems with drugs or alcohol.

- Choosing not to use drugs and staying away from alcohol until you're an adult keeps you healthy and makes it easier to do well in school, sports, and other activities. Doing drugs or drinking alcohol can keep you from being the best person you can be.

Why Do People Use Drugs and Alcohol?

ASK THE DOCTOR

Q: Are all drugs harmful to a person's health?

A: No, there are many drugs that can keep you healthy or make you better when you are sick. While almost all illegal drugs are harmful to your health, medicines are also a kind of drug. They aren't likely to make you sick or hurt your body. Make sure to always follow the instructions the doctor gives you or your parents so that you're using medicine in the way the doctor thinks is best.

There isn't any one thing that makes a person want to take drugs or drink alcohol. Both drugs and alcohol affect the mind and the body, changing the way a person thinks, feels, and understands the world. Many drugs affect the parts of the brain that control feeling good, leading people to feel what is called a "high." Alcohol also affects the way the brain works. It can make people feel different from normal.

People might take drugs or drink because they want to get away from problems in their lives, because they think drugs make them feel better, or because they just want to feel something different. A person who doesn't feel good about herself or her life might take drugs or drink to feel better. Drugs and alcohol don't make problems go away, though. They only cover up what is still there. They might even end up making the problems worse. Other kids might take drugs or drink to fit in with a group of people.

Some people have used drugs long enough that they are *addicted* to drugs and alcohol. A person's body wants more and more, even if he wants to stop taking drugs. Addiction makes it difficult to stop taking drugs or drinking alcohol.

What's Wrong with Using Drugs and Alcohol?

There are many different reasons not to use drugs or drink alcohol, especially for young people. Drugs and alcohol can harm your health, make it harder to make good decisions, and keep you from reaching your goals. Using drugs and alcohol can hurt your school work and grades. They can cause problems with your family and friends. Using drugs and

Words to Know

Dependent: if you or your body becomes dependent on something, that means that you need it or have a hard time going without it. Your body can become dependent on drugs and alcohol, meaning your body needs it or wants more to work normally.

drinking can even change for the worse the way you act and think about the world.

It's also important to know that young people are still developing. That means their bodies and minds haven't finished growing yet. When a young person uses drugs or drinks alcohol, she can harm the way her body and mind are growing, sometimes permanently.

Drugs and alcohol can also be addictive. That means that your body gets used to having the drug, or even *dependent* on it, making it hard to stop taking it.

Addiction to drugs or alcohol can really mess up your life! It makes you spend your money, keeps you from doing things you love, hurts your relationships with other people, and keeps you from succeeding in the ways you want.

My parents sometimes drink wine or beer. Does this mean they are going to have problems?

A: No, it's alright for adults to drink alcohol from time to time, as long as they don't drink too much or too often. It's important to know that alcohol affects young people and adults very differently. It's more important that kids and young people don't drink because their brains and bodies aren't fully grown. Alcohol can be harmful to their growth in many ways.

What Happens Inside Your Body If You Drink Alcohol?

When you drink wine, beer, or other types of alcoholic drinks, alcohol enters your blood through your stomach and intestines. This is the same for all food and drink. Once alcohol is in your blood, it begins to have an effect on your body and mind. Depending on how much alcohol is in your blood, the effects it has are different. The amount of alcohol in your blood is called *Blood Alcohol Content (BAC)*.

At first, alcohol may make you feel happy but also keep you from thinking completely clearly. You may also start having trouble moving properly. If you drink more, you may start to get sleepy, move more slowly, have trouble seeing straight, or lose your balance. Drink even more and you might start having more trouble thinking, speaking, and moving. After that, you may not be able to move at all, may fall down or throw up, and probably won't be able to walk. Keep drinking, and you will probably pass out, breathe more slowly, and could even die.

What Are Drugs?

Words to Know

Illegal: if something is illegal, it is against the law. Many drugs are illegal to buy, sell, and have. Drugs like cocaine and heroin are illegal.

A drug is anything that you put into your body that changes the way your mind or body works. There are drugs that are good for you, like medicines. Then there are drugs that are bad for you. Many of the drugs that are bad for you are not only harmful to your health but are also *illegal*. People use these illegal drugs to get a high that changes the way they feel or think. Illegal drugs like heroin, cocaine, and others can do damage to your body and keep you from being able to make smart decisions.

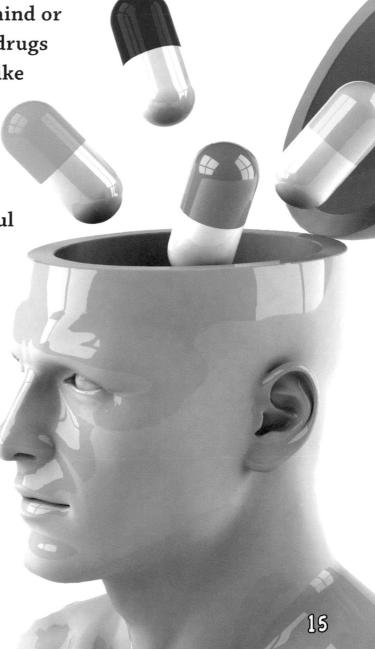

What Are Amphetamines?

Amphetamines are a type of drug called a stimulant. Stimulants speed up the way the body works. They can make people feel more awake or like they have more energy. Amphetamines are sometimes used as medicine by doctors. Someone with ADHD might be given a kind of amphetamine to help him focus.

Amphetamines can also be *abused,* though. Abusing amphetamines can be very dangerous. Someone who uses amphetamines may start to have problems with the way she thinks. A person who uses amphetamines a lot might start to have trouble sleeping, have thoughts of hurting others, or even see things that aren't really there.

Words to Know

Abused: abusing a drug means taking too much or using it in a way it was not meant to be used.

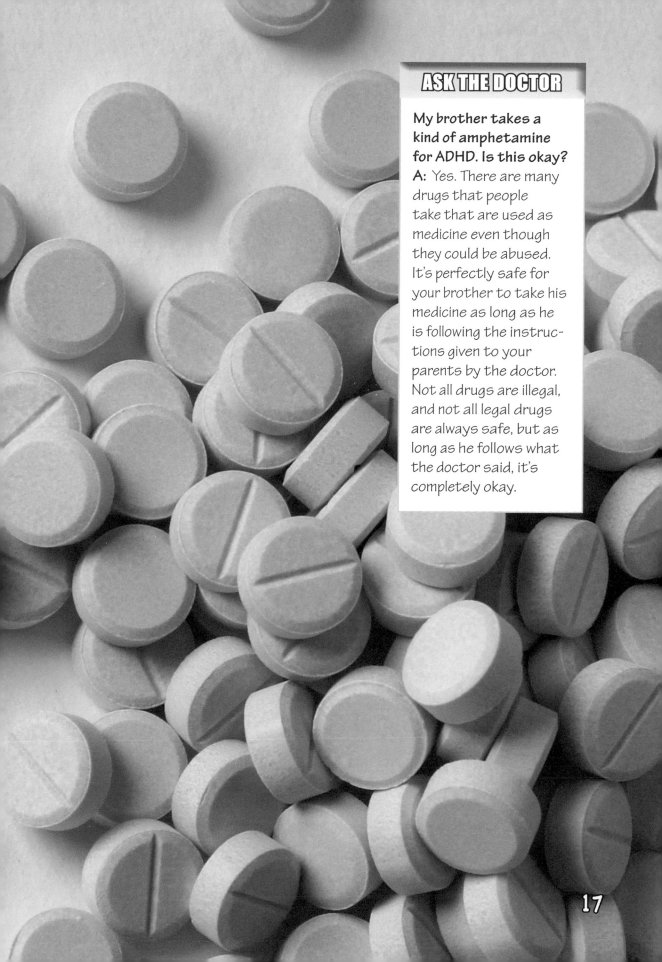

ASK THE DOCTOR

My brother takes a kind of amphetamine for ADHD. Is this okay?

A: Yes. There are many drugs that people take that are used as medicine even though they could be abused. It's perfectly safe for your brother to take his medicine as long as he is following the instructions given to your parents by the doctor. Not all drugs are illegal, and not all legal drugs are always safe, but as long as he follows what the doctor said, it's completely okay.

What Are Cocaine and Crack?

Cocaine is a very addictive drug that looks like powder. It is breathed in through the nose (also known as *snorting* or sniffing). Cocaine, like amphetamines, is a powerful stimulant that can speed up the minds and bodies of users. The drug is also very addictive, and users will often need to do more and more to get the high they want, making cocaine very dangerous.

Crack is a kind of cocaine that is smoked. Crack looks like a crystal or a rock. Like cocaine, crack is very addictive.

Cocaine and crack give users an intense high that makes people feel happy, energetic, and excited. But that rush doesn't last, and when it's over, the user will feel very tired and very sad. Often, that makes a user want more cocaine, which may lead to an addiction to the drug. Cocaine users will also need more of the drug to get the same effect, putting them at risk of addiction and harming their health.

Words to Know

Snorting: many drugs that come in powder form are snorted, meaning that they are breathed in through the nose.

Both cocaine and crack can badly damage your body. Using cocaine can harm your heart in many ways, and even cause a deadly heart attack.

What About Cough Medicines?

You've probably taken cough medicine to keep yourself from coughing when you're sick. Whether in syrup or pill form, cough medicine contains a drug that helps you control your coughing. It is called dextromethorphan or DXM. This drug can be used as a medicine to help you feel better, but, like many others, it can also be abused. The same drug in cough medicine that keeps you from coughing can also be used to to get high.

Most people take DXM by drinking a lot of cough syrup or taking a lot of cough medicine that comes in pill form. Some drink as many as three or four bottles of cough syrup!

Abusing cough medicine causes feelings of confusion, *hallucinations*, and changes in the way a person understands their senses (like touch and hearing). Users can also have problems moving and speaking properly. Because people abusing DXM in cough medicine have to take a lot to get the high they want, they are also taking in dangerous amounts

Did You Know?

Now that people have started abusing cough syrup, many stores will not sell some kinds of medicine to young people under the age of eighteen.

Words to Know

Hallucinations: when you see or hear something that isn't really there.

of the other medicines that are in cough medicine. Medicines that aren't normally dangerous can cause health problems if taken in large amounts.

Using cough medicine can lead to addiction to DXM. Taking a combination of DXM and other drugs like alcohol or some kinds of pills can be especially dangerous, or even deadly.

What Is Ecstasy?

ASK THE DOCTOR

Is it safe to use ecstasy once, or just once in a while?

A: No. Even trying ecstasy one time can be harmful to your health. Ecstasy changes the way your brain works, making it harder to think straight and feel things normally. Even with just one use, the drug can also cause your body to heat up to dangerous levels by affecting the part of the brain that keeps your body temperature normal.

Ecstasy is a drug that looks like a pill. The drug is usually swallowed, but sometimes pills are crushed and then snorted like cocaine. Ecstasy makes people feel very happy and also changes the way they understand the world around them. They might get more feeling from the things they touch or feel emotions very strongly. The drug also gives users many of the same effects as stimulants like amphetamine or cocaine. They may feel more *energized* or more awake, for example. The drug can cause confusion, *depression*, and problems with sleep. It will also make the user want more and more ecstasy. Ecstasy affects the part of the brain that allows a person to feel good, and it can sometimes damage this part of the brain, keeping people from feeling as good as they do when on the drug. This damage may be permanent.

Ecstasy causes many of the same problems as stimulants like cocaine. It causes problems with the heart, liver, and kidneys because the drug can heat a person's body up to dangerous temperatures. Ecstasy can also cause serious *dehydration*. Unlike many other drugs, ecstasy stays in the body for a long time. If people take ecstasy often, they may have more of the drug in their body than they know.

Words to Know

Energized: having lots of energy or having the urge to be very active.

Depression: depression is a type of deep sadness that lasts for a very long time.

Dehydration: dehydration means a person doesn't have enough water in his body.

What Is Heroin?

Heroin is a drug that looks like powder. It also comes in a form called "black tar" that is dark and sticky. Heroin is taken by breathing it in through the nose, smoking it, or   it with a needle. Heroin is a very

addictive drug. Just one use can start a person on a path toward addiction. When someone takes heroin, he feels very happy and very sleepy. Using heroin can also make it hard to move normally. Taking too much of a powerful drug, called an overdose, can be deadly.

Words to Know

Injecting: something that is injected is put into the blood through a needle. Drugs like heroin are taken by injecting them straight into the blood.

What Kinds of Drugs Are Sniffed?

When you think of drugs that people use in ways that aren't for health, you may think of illegal drugs. But there are also many household items meant for cleaning or cooking that can be abused like other drugs.

These drugs are called inhalants, meaning that you take them by breathing them in. Vegetable cooking spray, some types of glue, cans of whipped cream, and nail polish remover are just some of the things that some people abuse as drugs. By breathing in these products, or the gases they give off, a person can feel high. However, this practice is very dangerous. These products contain many dangerous chemicals, which can harm the brain in many ways. They can make it hard to think, move, or see normally. Inhalant use can cause problems with a user's mood, making him angry or depressed. They can also harm the heart as well, and even cause deadly heart attacks. Even a healthy young person can die from using inhalants just once.

Did You Know?

Inhalant abuse is a global problem. Youth around the world turn to inhalents to get high. India, Europe, Southeast Asia, North America, and First Nations (native) communities in Canada all have high rates of abuse.

ASK THE DOCTOR

Are the cleaning or cooking products people abuse as inhalants dangerous when used correctly?
A: No, they aren't. Using these products in the way that they were meant to be will keep you safe from the dangerous effects they can have on people who abuse them. Make sure to follow instructions on the can or package, and you won't have any of the problems caused by inhalant abuse.

What Is LSD?

LSD is a type of drug called a hallucinogen. Hallucinogens cause users to have what are called hallucinations. Using drugs that cause hallucinations can be very dangerous. Think about it: if you aren't seeing things around you clearly, you might miss something that could hurt you. Normally, you would have seen the danger right away.

LSD is sometimes also called acid. The drug is taken as a pill, liquid, or soaked into a sugar cube. Sometimes, a drop of liquid is placed on a piece of paper and swallowed. The drug changes a user's mood and can make her start to see things that aren't there within the first hour of taking it. Someone on LSD may see the color, shape, size, or movement of things differently from someone not using the drug. The hallucinations caused by LSD can also make users feel something that isn't there or change the way they understand their own senses. Because LSD affects the way people understand the world

Did You Know?

LSD was first created by a chemist in Switzerland who didn't know its effect on people until he accidentally took some five years after creating it. Thirty years later, many countries began making the drug illegal.

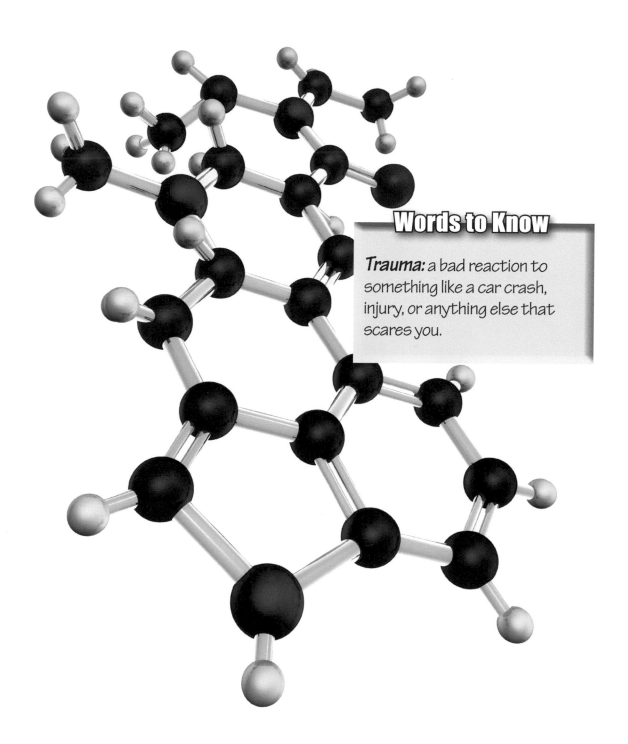

Words to Know

Trauma: a bad reaction to something like a car crash, injury, or anything else that scares you.

around them, it's easy for LSD users to accidentally hurt themselves. The drug changes the way users see what is real, making it hard to make good decisions while using it. An overdose of LSD can lead to longer hallucinations or cause psychological *trauma*.

What Is Marijuana?

Words to Know

Cancer: cancer is the name for many diseases that all have to do with cells in the body growing out of control. Cancer can make people very sick or even die.

Marijuana is a drug that comes from a plant. Marijuana is smoked in a pipe or in a cigarette, which is sometimes called a joint. The drug can also be made into tea or mixed into foods.

Marijuana affects the mind and the body. It can make people feel happy or giggly, but it also makes it hard to remember clearly or make decisions. Using marijuana can affect people's ability to learn, makes it harder to solve problems, and keeps users from being able to move as well as they could when not using the drug. Marijuana can cause confusion and slow reactions, and makes people anxious. Using marijuana a lot can also make it harder for people to concentrate and makes them lose interest in the things they once enjoyed.

Smoking marijuana is also dangerous for many of the same reasons as smoking cigarettes. Smoking causes problems with the lungs, including diseases that make it harder to breathe, and can lead to lung, mouth, and throat *cancer*.

What Is Meth?

Meth is short for methamphetamine. Methamphetamine is a type of amphetamine that affects the body and mind more quickly than normal amphetamines. Meth comes in different forms and is used in many ways. It

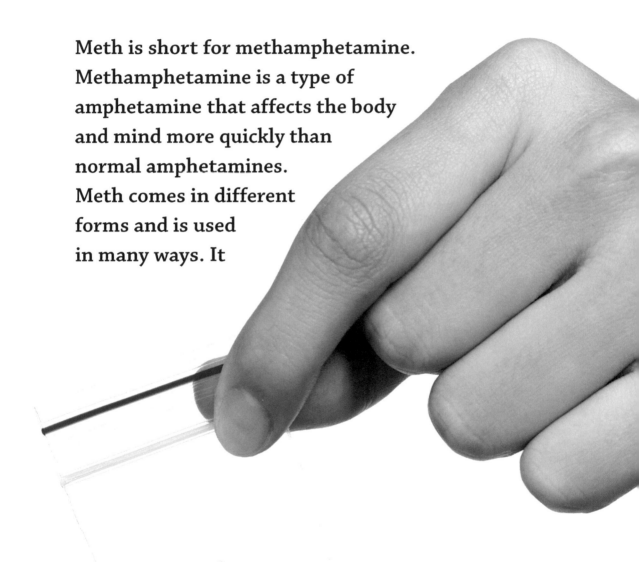

can look like a pill or a powder. It can be injected, swallowed, or breathed in through the nose. Crystal meth is a hard, rock-like type of meth that is smoked in a pipe.

Meth gives the user a quick burst of energy and a good feeling when smoked or injected. When meth is taken in pill form or breathed in through the nose, the high can last longer. Meth is very addictive, especially the more times a person uses the drug.

Meth can make users angry or even make them *violent* or confused. Users can start to see or hear things that aren't there. Some people even start to feel like bugs are crawling under their skin!

Using meth can make it hard to sleep. It leads to a loss of *appetite*, causes teeth problems, and damages the brain. Using meth can also raise body temperature, even causing death because of overheating.

ASK THE DOCTOR

What kinds of teeth problems does meth cause?

A: Meth can cause a person to damage or even lose her teeth. Someone who uses meth very often will grind her teeth together, which badly damages teeth over time. Meth also causes a person's mouth to become very dry, which can harm her teeth. Meth users often don't care for their teeth in the ways a person should, making their problems worse.

Are Prescription Drugs Safe?

Prescription drugs are the drugs that your doctor gives you to keep you healthy or make you better when you are sick. Only a doctor can give out prescriptions for drugs that are used as medicine. These drugs are safe when used the way the doctor tells you to. Following the instructions your doctor gives you when she tells you to take a medicine is very important. It will keep you safe and make sure that the medicine doesn't hurt you.

Words to Know

Prescription: a prescription is a note given to a pharmacist from a doctor that explains to a patient what medicine to take and how to take it.

Did You Know?

High schoolers are most likely to abuse painkillers, medicines that help patients deal with pain. Two out of five teens in the United States alone say they know someone who has abused prescription painkillers.

Taking a prescription drug that you shouldn't be using can be just as dangerous as taking illegal drugs. Just like any other drug, prescription drugs can be abused. Drugs like painkillers can be taken to get high even though they are legal and given out by doctors. Using these drugs in the way your doctor says you should keeps you safe, but abusing prescription medicines can lead to addiction and many health problems. Take too much of these drugs and they can even lead to death.

What About Cigarettes?

In the same way that alcohol is a legal drug, cigarettes are also a drug that can be bought by adults. Cigarettes contain a drug called nicotine. The drug is very addictive, so that people get hooked on smoking cigarettes.

Nicotine makes users feel relaxed and even happy, but it doesn't last very long. Smoking also has a very negative effect on a smoker's health. Smoking cigarettes can cause major problems with a person's breathing, including *emphysema*. A person who smokes will also be more likely to have a heart attack than someone who doesn't. Smoking can cause lung, throat, and mouth cancer. These forms of cancer are particularly deadly. People may smoke because it makes them feel good for a little while, but cigarettes are very dangerous to their health.

Words to Know

Emphysema: a long-term disease of the lungs that makes it very hard to breathe normally.

ASK THE DOCTOR

Are electronic cigarettes safer than regular cigarettes?
A: Because electronic cigarettes are such a new product, there hasn't been as much research on their effect as there has been on the effects of regular cigarettes. Many experts believe, however, that electronic cigarettes are just as harmful as regular cigarettes because they still give the smoker nicotine, an addictive drug. The U.S. government has said that e-cigarettes are harmful to health.

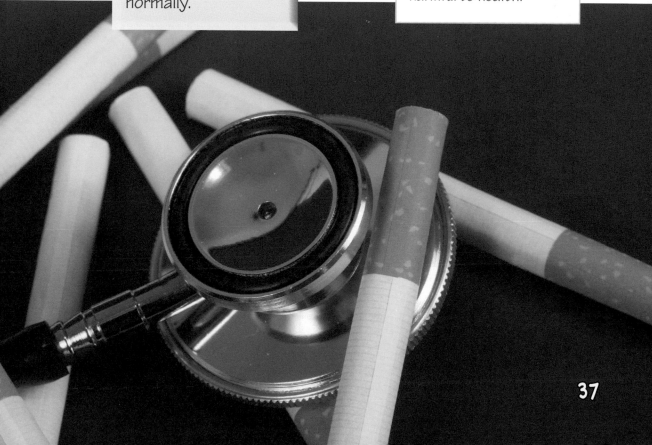

How Can You Tell If You Have a Problem with Drugs or Alcohol?

Drugs and alcohol can change your life in many negative ways. They affect your health and the way you get along with others.

There are many signs that point to a problem with drugs or drinking. You might have a problem with drugs or alcohol if:

- you need to use or drink more and more to get the same feeling.
- you get sick when you don't use drugs or drink.
- you spend a lot of your time using or trying to get drugs.
- you continue to use drugs even when you know the problems they cause.
- you lose interest in activities you once enjoyed doing.
- you have trouble quitting drinking alcohol or using drugs, even after trying to quit a few times.

Did You Know?

Talking to a professional who understands drug and alcohol problems (like a counselor or social worker) can be a good way to find out if you have a problem with drugs or alcohol. Many school counselors can help you as well.

What Is Addiction?

Addiction is when your body has gotten used to having a drug or alcohol in its system. Because the body is used to the drug, it starts to expect it to be there. If you use drugs, your body may start to *crave* the drug, leading you to feel like you want more of it, or like you need to take it.

Addiction is a very difficult thing to control. An addict may not want to take drugs or drink but feels sick or sad when he doesn't. He may take drugs or drink to avoid feeling bad when he isn't drinking or doing drugs. An addiction to drugs or alcohol can take over a person's life, making her start to ignore everything except getting and taking more. She chases the feeling that the drug gives her because she begins to feel that taking drugs or drinking is the only way she can feel "normal." Soon, an addict's life is centered around

Words to Know

Crave: if someone craves something, he wants it very badly, and even feels like he needs it to feel good.

drugs or alcohol, leaving little room for much else. An addict can lose friends, stop being interested in the activities he once loved, or start spending all of his time and money on drugs or alcohol.

What Are the Warning Signs of Addiction?

So how can you tell if you or someone close to you may have an addiction to drugs or alcohol? There are many signs that point to addiction. A user might be addicted to drugs or alcohol if she:

- Uses drugs or drinks when alone.
- Gets drunk or high all the time.
- Lies about drugs or alcohol.
- Tries to get other people to drink or use drugs.
- Needs to drink or use drugs to handle problems in her life or to have a good time.
- Has stolen money to use for drugs or alcohol.
- Goes to school drunk or high.
- Thinks ahead about getting drunk or high.
- Doesn't care about things she used to care about (school, sports, arts, hanging out with friends, etc.).
- Starts only hanging out with friends who use drugs or drink.

What Should You Do If You Think a Friend Has a Problem with Drugs or Alcohol?

Addiction to drugs or alcohol doesn't just affect the person who is addicted. It can also affect the people around that person. Many young people who use drugs say that they would talk to a friend about their problem.

If you decide to talk to a friend who is using drugs, make sure you go about it in the right way. Don't talk to your friend about his problem while he is high or drunk. Pick a place and time to talk that is private, so you don't embarrass your friend in front of others. Try to give your friend your support, instead of getting mad at him for his problem. Talk to your friend about how drugs are affecting his life and your friendship with him. Be sure to talk about how much you care about him and what having his friendship means to

Did You Know?

Alcoholism and drug addiction are diseases, not choices. Some people may be more at risk for these diseases if their parents or other family members also had them.

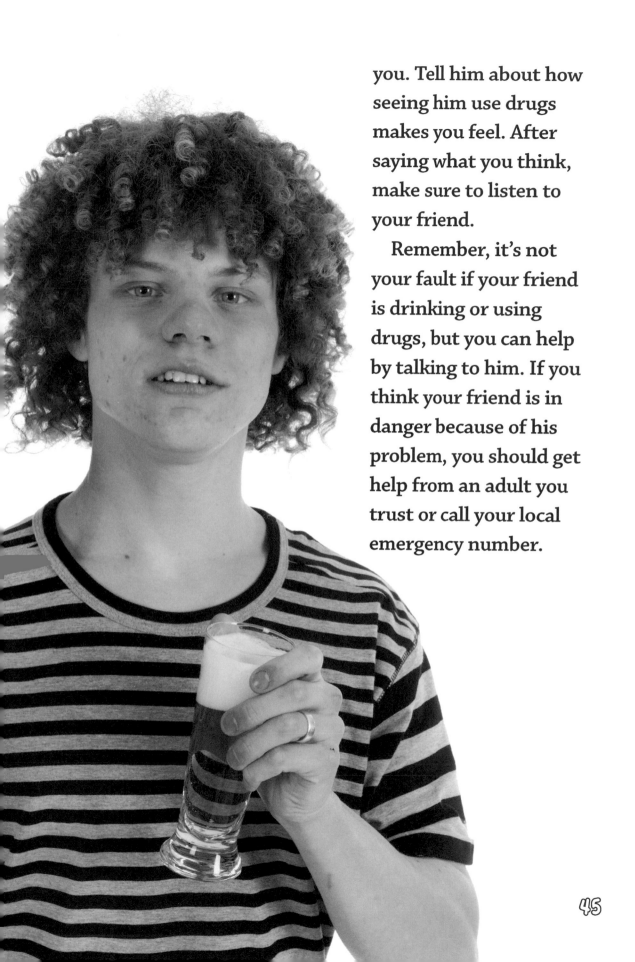

you. Tell him about how seeing him use drugs makes you feel. After saying what you think, make sure to listen to your friend.

Remember, it's not your fault if your friend is drinking or using drugs, but you can help by talking to him. If you think your friend is in danger because of his problem, you should get help from an adult you trust or call your local emergency number.

What If Someone in Your Family Has a Problem with Drugs or Alcohol?

If someone in your family is abusing drugs or alcohol, it's important that you know that their drug use is not your fault. If your brother, sister, or parent is using drugs, you shouldn't feel that they are using drugs because of anything you've done. You should also know that having a problem with drugs or alcohol, or even an addiction, doesn't make a person bad or weak. Many addicts wish they could stop using drugs or alcohol but have lost control over their habit. Beating an addiction to drugs or alcohol isn't easy. If a parent is using drugs in your house and drug use is making your home unsafe, you need to talk to an adult you trust. Whether you choose a teacher, relative, or family friend, it's important that you are safe. In some cases, you may be able to talk honestly to a family member who is using drugs or alcohol about what drug or alcohol use has done to your relationship. If the family member who has a problem decides to get treatment, make sure you give her your support. You can't control her, but you can make sure to support her when she seeks help.

Where Can You Get Help?

Addiction to drugs or alcohol can be a very difficult thing to handle. But there are many ways to get help if you or someone you know has a problem. Remember that you aren't alone if you or someone close to you has a problem with drugs or alcohol. You can get help at your school, from a school counselor or social worker. These people are there to help young people with all sorts of problems, including addiction, drug and alcohol abuse, and problems with friends or family. They are trained in how to talk about a lot of different problems and will know how to help. Counselors and social workers can also give you advice or help without talking to others about your problems. That means you can trust them to help you without telling someone else about your troubles, even your parents. There are also many other places to turn for help with addiction to drugs or alcohol.

Telling people you trust that you are quitting using drugs, drinking, or smoking cigarettes can give you a better chance of staying away from those things. Having the support of people who care about you can really help.

Treatment for Alcoholism

Like many other drugs, alcohol can be addictive. An addiction to alcohol is called alcoholism. An addiction to alcohol is a very serious thing, but there are many ways an alcoholic can get help for the problem. Treatment comes in many different forms, and many people have gotten help and beaten their addiction.

If you or someone close to you has an addiction to alcohol, there are many ways to get treatment. Support groups like Alcoholics Anonymous (also called AA or Al Anon for short) can be a great place to get help for addiction from other people who have been through it before and beaten alcoholism themselves. Programs like AA and others can be a great place to seek help after an alcoholic stops drinking too.

An alcoholic can also change her behavior, the way she acts and the things she does, so that she doesn't do the things that led to becoming addicted in the first place. Treatments that work on the behavior of an alcoholic can help the person to understand why she is an addict, and help her change the way she thinks about alcohol and herself.

Another way to treat alcoholism is to use medicine. Some medicines used to treat alcoholism lessen the effect of alcohol, or make an alcoholic who drinks sick. An alcoholic who takes these medicines will want to drink less, but the medicines don't work after an alcoholic stops drinking. Many treatments use medicine, counseling, and changes in behavior to help alcoholics stop drinking—and make sure they don't start again.

Treatment for Drug Addiction

Just as there are treatments for alcoholism, there are many ways to beat an addiction to drugs. First, it's important for someone who is addicted to drugs to find an expert to talk to. An expert can help a drug addict figure out what kind of treatment will work best based on how serious the addiction is. The expert may suggest counseling for the addict, so she can understand why it is that she turned to drugs and work to get better so that drugs aren't needed in the future. The expert may suggest a support group with other drug addicts, so that the addict has people to talk to who understand what he's going through. The expert may also recommend that an addict go through what is called rehabilitation, or rehab. Going to rehab usually means spending time at a place that understands addiction and how to help people get past it. Rehab centers have doctors, nurses, and counselors whose job it is to help people beat addiction and learn to live without drugs.

Did You Know?

While taking drugs is something users choose to do, being addicted takes that choice away from them. Addicts no longer have control over their drug use.

Treatment for Nicotine Addiction

If you or someone you know is addicted to the nicotine in cigarettes, there are many ways you can quit smoking. For many people, quitting can be difficult to do alone, depending only on willpower. Many of these smokers can get help from what are called nicotine replacement treatments. These treatments can help a smoker feel less like he needs a cigarette by giving him a small amount of nicotine without smoking. Treatments like these are found in many drug stores and come in gum or patch forms (as well as others). Using nicotine gum can help stop a person's craving for cigarettes and help her quit over time.

Along with nicotine-replacement treatments, smokers need to change the way they think about smoking. Figuring out ways to deal with *stress* or feeling down other than smoking is one big step toward quitting. Getting support from friends or family is also very important. Knowing that people are rooting for them to quit helps a lot!

If you smoke, quitting and beating an addiction to nicotine can help keep your heart, lungs, and other organs healthy. It might be hard to do, but quitting is the best thing for your health. It will also keep your teeth whiter, your breath fresher, and your clothes smelling better!

Words to Know

Stress: worry that happens as a result of a demanding experience, like a test, a fight with a friend, or family problems.

You're Worth It!

Drugs and alcohol can get in the way of reaching your goals. No matter what you want to do with your life, drugs and alcohol make it harder to succeed. They can keep you from being the best friend you can be. They can hurt your relationship with your parents. Drugs and alcohol can affect how you do in school, how well you play sports, how creative you can be, and how you think about the world around you.

Taking drugs or drinking alcohol is a choice. People around you may want you to drink or use drugs, but you don't have to if you don't want to. Make sure that you are being true to who you are, and not following someone else on a path you don't want to go down. Just because friends of yours are making the decision to use drugs or drink, doesn't mean you have to do the same.

Using drugs or drinking alcohol can have serious consequences for young people. They can harm your health, waste your money, and keep you from focusing on the things you love to do. Think about it: you can't save up for the things you want if you're spending all your money on drugs. You can't enjoy being a teenager if you're arrested for drinking at an early age. You can't be the star of a sports team with a drug addiction. Always remember that those things are worth more than drugs and alcohol.

Alby was 13 when he first tried smoking marijuana. A friend offered him some while they were hanging out. Alby didn't want to turn his friend down because he didn't want to seem uncool. He felt he had to try smoking marijuana so that he could fit in with others. Alby also wanted to get away from his problems. His parents were drug addicts and Alby was raised in foster homes and by his grandmother. He was mad at the world.

After Alby first tried marijuana, he kept using the drug. It made his problems seem far away. But Alby's problems weren't gone. Marijuana made his problems worse. He smoked marijuna every day for the next five years. Alby couldn't focus at school because he was high all the time. Soon, he left high school and started selling drugs so he could smoke more. It wasn't long before Alby's drug sales got him arrested. He ended up going to jail.

After counseling, Alby is working on getting his life back together. He stopped smoking and is working through his problems without drugs. Alby knows marijuana made his life harder.

Find Out More

Above the Influence
www.abovetheinfluence.com

Drug Abuse Resistance Education (D.A.R.E.)
www.dare.com

KidsHealth.org: What You Need to Know About Drugs
www.kidshealth.org/kid/grow/drugs_alcohol/know_
drugs.html

Scholastic—Heads Up: Real News About Drugs and Your
Body
headsup.scholastic.com

Taking it Global
issues.tigweb.org/substance

World Health Organization—Alcohol
www.who.int/topics/alcohol_drinking/en

World Health Organization—Drug Abuse
www.who.int/topics/substance_abuse/en

Index

Picture Credits

About the Author

Chance Parker has written many books for young adults and children. He lives in Minneapolis, Minnesota in the United States.

About the Consultant

Elise DeVore Berlan, MD, MPH, FAAP, is a faculty member of the Division of Adolescent Health at Nationwide Children's Hospital and an Assistant Professor of Clinical Pediatrics at the Ohio State University College of Medicine. She completed her fellowship in adolescent medicine at Children's Hospital Boston and obtained a master's degree in public health at the Harvard School of Public Health. Dr. Berlan completed her residency in pediatrics at the Children's Hospital of Philadelphia, where she also served an additional year as chief resident. She received her medical degree from the University of Iowa College of Medicine.

CPSIA information can be obtained
at www.ICGtesting.com
Printed in the USA
LVIC06n1047021216
515500LV00003B/3